GUADALCANAL

ENLIST NOW
U.S. MARINE CORPS

THIS IS
GUADALCANAL

The Original Combat Photography

L. Douglas Keeney
William S. Butler

Quill
William Morrow
New York

Copyright © 1998 by L. Douglas Keeney
and William S. Butler

All rights reserved. No part of this book may
be reproduced or utilized in any form or by
any means, electronic or mechanical,
including photocopying, recording, or by
any information storage or retrieval system,
without permission in writing from the
Publisher. Inquiries should be addressed to:
Permissions Department
William Morrow and Company, Inc.,
1350 Avenue of the Americas, New York,
N.Y. 10019.

It is the policy of William Morrow and
Company, Inc., and its imprints and affili-
ates, recognizing the importance of preserv-
ing what has been written, to print the
books we publish on acid-free paper, and
we exert our best efforts to that end.

Library of Congress Cataloging-in-Publica-
tion Data has been applied for.

ISBN 0-688-17081-1

Printed in the United States of America

1 2 3 4 5 6 7 8 9 10

BOOK DESIGN BY AVION PARK

www.williammorrow.com

L. Douglas Keeney and William S. Butler have co-authored five books, including *Day of Destiny: The Photographs of D-Day*, *Tragedy at Sea* and *No Easy Days: The Incredible Drama of Naval Aviation*. They share an interest in military history and reside in Louisville, Kentucky.

It is our privilege to remember the brave men who fought on Guadalcanal. To those who helped us complete this photographic history, we extend our thanks:

Jane O'Boyle
Michael Murphy
Zach Schisgal
Mark Forman
Jill Johnson Keeney
Joe Bohn
Roby Doan

All photographs and oral histories, except where indicated, are from the record groups of the U.S. Marine Corps, the U.S. Navy, the Army Signal Corps, the U.S. Coast Guard and the U.S. Air Force, held at National Archives II, College Park, Maryland.

(Left) The rainy season in the South Pacific dumped huge volumes of water into U.S. encampments, flooding tents, kitchens, roads and hospitals, making life even more miserable for combat-weary GIs.

As night fell on Guadalcanal, everything changed. The jungle, by day evenly divided between blue sky and green earth, was transformed into a foreboding world cloaked in utter blackness, a place too dark, too mysterious, and that seemed indescribably evil and possessed. It was also a transforming time for the Japanese. On Guadalcanal, the night belonged to the enemy, picking their way through the dense foliage, visually probing the blackness to make out a foxhole, then raising up in a frenzied charge, the screeching yell of "Banzai!" shattering the still, night air. Those who experienced these sudden, fanatical assaults would never forget them, nor their time in this hellish corner of the world.

—L. Douglas Keeney, William S. Butler

CONTENTS

(Left) American P-400s and P-39s were among the first fighters to be based at Henderson Field, Guadalcanal.

INTRODUCTION

The Battle of Guadalcanal was a grueling, six-month struggle on land, in the air, and at sea, to oust the Japanese Imperial forces from the Solomon Islands. It was more than a battle over a chain of islands in the Pacific. Guadalcanal was the crucible of American and Japanese military traditions. It was a trial of withering machine gun fire against waves of soldiers brandishing gun and sword, with soldiers encountering an adversary that fought at night. It turned into one of the fiercest battles of World War II.

As Japan island-hopped toward Australia, America saw the Solomons as the place to draw the line. Further, from these islands the U.S. could build a series of naval bases across the Pacific to support an eventual attack on Japan. The original objective had been to land on an island in the Solomons called Tulagi, but then the Japanese started building a fighter strip on the larger island of Guadalcanal. The American command knew the Japanese had to be stopped from establishing this strategic airbase, and wanted to take control of Guadalcanal for themselves. They would transform this island into an "unsinkable aircraft carrier."

The Marines landed on Guadalcanal on August 7, 1942, scattering the enemy into the jungle. On Tulagi, they met bitter resistence but recaptured the small island the next day. Knowing that the Japanese would fight to dislodge them, the Marines set their perimeter around the Guadalcanal airfield renamed Henderson Field. Henderson would be the focus of the battles to follow for the next six months.

Humiliated by their defeat at Midway, the Japanese preferred dying over surrender and they were determined not to lose Guadalcanal. The enemy's capacity for killing startled the young, inexperienced Marines. Constantly damp from rain, sweat, and the fetid muck, Americans nonetheless found the humidity of day preferable to the deadly assaults at night by the frenzied Japanese soldiers.

Since this battleground was isolated by vast stretches of the Pacific Ocean, vicious naval battles were fought as each side attempted to stop the resupply transports. American ships were, at first, devastated by night attacks and the superior Japanese torpedoes. On the carriers, if the relentless shelling wasn't enough, there were the kamikazes. American ground forces, knee-deep in mud, encountered warriors wielding bayonets, machetes, and nerves of cold steel. As James Jones wrote in his gut-wrenching autobiographical novel, *The Thin Red Line*: "They had been initiated into a strange, insane, twilight fraternity where explanation would be forever impossible."

Darkness intensified the jungle environment and deadly

Marines swim a .30 caliber machine gun across the Matanikau River. The banks of the Matanikau were the site of numerous engagements. The river was west of Henderson Field.

zeal of the enemy. Nearly every battle took place at night. Exploding shells, torpedoes, grenades, machine guns and bombs painted the heavens with an eerie glow, night after night. Even without the rainstorms, mosquitoes and racking fevers, few would have slept during their long nights on Guadalcanal.

Guadalcanal was the first, and perhaps only, battle of World War II that combined assaults on the ground, at sea, in the skies and between aircraft carriers. The American forces confronted naval destroyers, jungle warfare, aerial dogfights, submarines, torpedoes, grenades, barbed wire and bare hands. On all fronts this beautiful tropical island was a hellish nightmare. Disease was widespread, and wounds festered beneath rotting bandages, killing large numbers outside of battle. Others simply went into shock, or, worse, insane.

Americans sent a total of 60,000 troops to Guadalcanal under "Operation Watchtower," between August, 1942 and February, 1943. The 1st Marine Division was there the longest, four grueling months, and Guadalcanal remains one of the defining campaigns in the history of the Marine Corps.

More than 1,600 American ground forces were killed, and nearly triple that number were lost at sea. The Japanese lost more than 25,000 troops on the island, and uncounted more on sunken ships. Both sides lost dozens of warships, several carriers, and hundreds of airplanes.

There have been few military campaigns of this magnitude, and Guadalcanal was the first in history to be im-

mortalized on camera. Much of the night action is necessarily missing from these pages. But the vivid war images presented here, captured by combat photographers, are eyewitness to the legendary, pivotal battle that changed the course of the war in the Pacific.

★ ★ ★

Photos tell only a small part of the incredible, true story of Guadalcanal. In addition to James Jones' *The Thin Red Line*, and the films of the same name, we recommend *Guadalcanal Diary* by Richard Tregaskis, and *Guadalcanal: The Definitive Account of the Landmark Battle* by Richard B. Frank. Mr. Frank's superb work helped resolve a great number of factual issues, and to him we are indebted.

Although the fighting was almost constant, historians have found it more convenient to understand Guadalcanal by organizing it along the lines of the major battles. We have followed this convention and chronicle the four major land battles—Tenaru, Edson's Ridge, Henderson Field and Guadalcanal—as well as the five major naval engagements—Savo Island, Eastern Solomons, Cape Esperance, Guadalcanal and Tassafaronga.

"Uncommon valor was a common virtue," Admiral Chester William Nimitz would later proclaim about the Marines at Iwo Jima. This was the valor forged at Guadalcanal. Most battles lost are only half as wretched as this battle won.

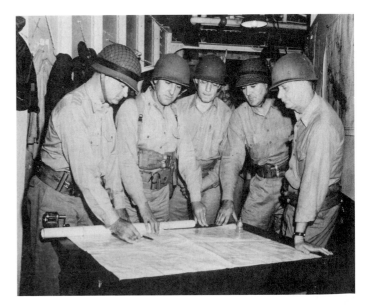

Marine officers hold an impromptu staff meeting prior to the Guadalcanal landing. Left to right are Maj. Gen. Alexander Vandegrift, who commanded the forces on Guadalcanal, Lt. Col. Gerald Thomas, Lt. Col. Randolph Pate, Col. Frank Goettge and Col. William James.

GUADALCANAL

Twenty thousand American Marines poured over the sides of Navy transports and onto the beaches of Guadalcanal. Before them towered the dense jungles of the South Pacific, complete with deadly spiders and snakes, crocodiles, swarms of malarious mosquitoes, and a rain forest canopy that could turn day into night and night into eternal darkness. It was a long way from home.

Largest in a chain of Pacific islands known as the Solomons, Guadalcanal sits just north of the equator. Not only surrounded by water but also drenched by monsoons in the spring and thunderstorms in the fall, Guadalcanal is hot, humid, and always wet.

Just 90 miles long and 25 miles wide, most of the habitable areas are on the coastal plains along the northeast, facing the islands of Florida, Tulagi and Savo. It was there that the battles of Guadalcanal were fought—on land, in the air, and in the deceptively beautiful blue waters offshore.

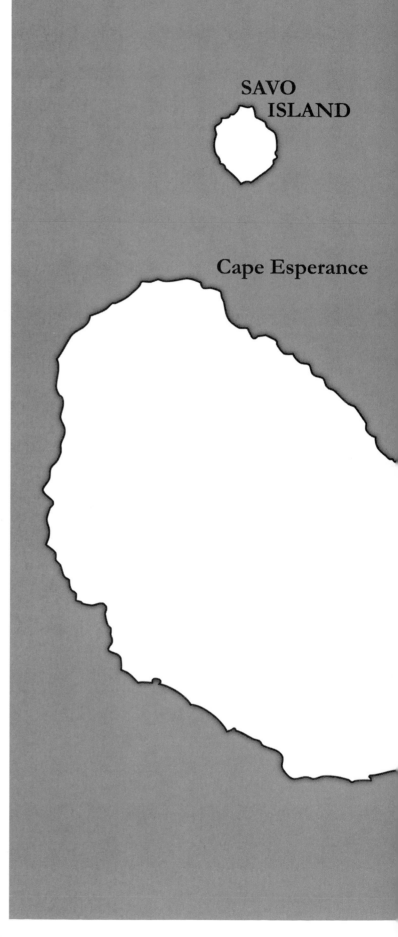

SAVO ISLAND

Cape Esperance

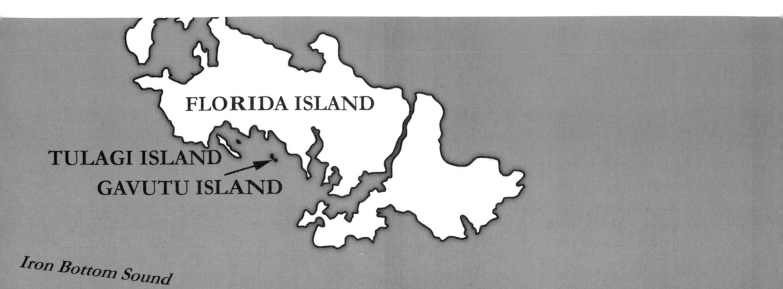

FLORIDA ISLAND

TULAGI ISLAND
GAVUTU ISLAND

Iron Bottom Sound

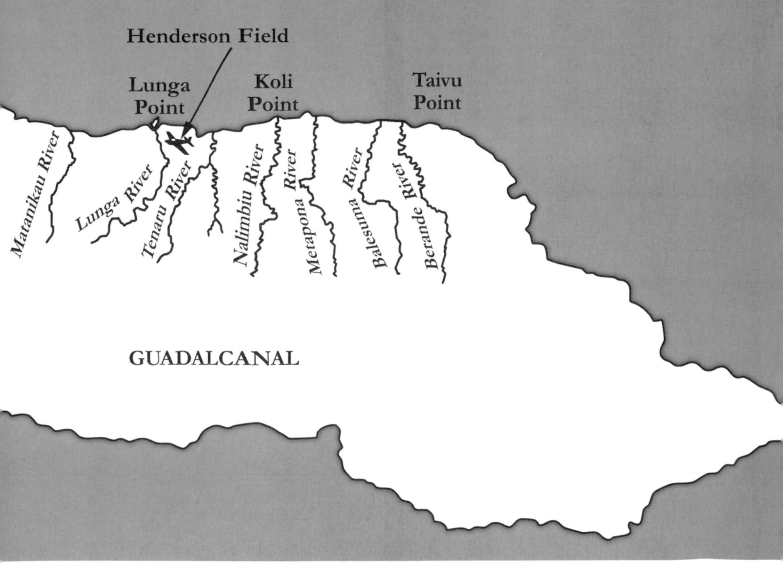

Henderson Field

Lunga
Point

Koli
Point

Taivu
Point

Matanikau River

Lunga River

Tenaru River

Nalimbiu River

Metapona River

Balesuma River

Berande River

GUADALCANAL

7 AUGUST 1942
THE INVASION

Before the landings, U.S. Marines tend to last-minute details and try to relax aboard their transports. Weapons are checked, card games are played, and letters from home are read one last time.

The 1st Marine Division was the main landing force of the South Pacific Amphibious Force, and had been hastily thrown together from many different Marine elements. Marine commanders, knowing the uneven training that had preceded the landings, were unsure of the soldiers' readiness.

These Marines don't know quite what to expect on the beaches of Guadalcanal, but their faces are anxious. Tripod-mounted .30 and .50 caliber machine guns like the one shown here would play an important role in the jungle battles, especially when enemy troops charged en masse toward Marine lines.

Zero hour, the time for the landing in Guadalcanal, was set at 0910. Debarkation was begun immediately under cover of ship's gunfire and air attack of the supporting carrier group. A favorable sea permitted use of cargo net gang-ways simultaneously on both sides of all ships. There was no noise or confusion attendant upon the operation and it proceeded with the smoothness and precision of a well-rehearsed, peace-time drill. All boats reached their correct beaches and debarked troops promptly and without casualties.

—Report of Major General Alexander Vandegrift, Commanding General, 1st Marine Division, following the landings on Guadalcanal

(Left and right) Marines in the first wave of landings jump from their boats and race across the beach toward the jungle. In these first landings Marines used landing craft without hinged front ramps; the only way out was over the side.

Marines did not know whether their landings would be opposed, but they weren't taking any chances. The first objective was to get out of the boats, dash across the beach, and melt into the jungle tree line, where squads could regroup.

(Left) Landing force Marines hustle into the tree line.

(Right) A tank climbs the beach dunes and looks for targets and driving lanes into the jungle.

Once ashore, wary, jumpy Marines look for the Japanese under every bush and in every hiding place.

A Marine patrol investigates a suspicious location along the shoreline. In a matter of minutes, Marines began to understand the Japanese had evacuated their camps.

192794

7 AUGUST
THE INVASION OF TULAGI

Three small islands near Guadalcanal–Tulagi, Gavutu and Tanambogo–were occupied by the Imperial Army. Of these, Tulagi was by far the most strategic and was also the most heavily defended. On this day, when Guadalcanal was simultaneously being invaded, Marine forces assaulted the beaches of Tulagi. Four hundred soldiers of the Imperial Army were there to repel them. After two days of bitter battle, the island had been taken by the Americans and had been declared "secure."

Across the channel from Guadalcanal lay the inhabited island of Tulagi and a garrison of Japanese soldiers. Above, as seen from the USS Chicago, *landing ships sit just offshore while bomb smoke signals the start of fighting. At right, a Japanese soldier is killed in one of the small, underground bunkers that dotted the island.*

Unlike Guadalcanal, the landings on the three main islands of the group—Tulagi, Gavutu and Tanambogo—were met with the most determined resistance of which the enemy was capable. Each of the three islands was a fort in itself, honey-combed with tunnels and caves, and thick with machine guns. Enemy positions could only be eliminated by bold action with grenades, well-placed explosives and submachine guns. The enemy employed the tricks for which he has become known, such as letting the points of units go through him, then firing on the main body. That night the enemy sortied and counter attacked, driving a wedge between C and A Companies of the Raiders, isolating C near the beach. The Marines had their first taste of the Jap at his best in a savage all-night fight with every means of deceiving an opponent employed.

—After-action report

It didn't take long for American Marines to realize that Japanese infantrymen had been trained to fight to the death. Against this kind of tenacity, Marines learned to make sure their opponents were dead before approaching the bodies.

There was no ease-in period for the Tulagi Marines. Acclimation to the jungle had to be immediate, and fighting was intense from the moment of the first landings. At right, wounded Marines are attended by corpsmen; one is carried out on a stretcher. Sniper fire hit all around as they walked.

The tenacity of the individual soldier was astonishing. Each Jap fought until he was killed himself rather than surrender. There were, it is estimated, about 500 Japanese on the island, and of these only three surrendered.

—General Alexander Vandegrift in his Tulagi after-action report

(Right and below) Invasion forces landed with little resistance and smoothly proceeded inland, but troubles loomed as the Marines turned to the daunting task of off-loading supplies. In addition to the normal difficulties of a beach landing, there were interruptions caused by two largely ineffective attacks by Japanese fighter-bombers, and the sheer size and volume of incoming shipments was overwhelming. By mid-afternoon, supplies were beginning to back up on the beaches. By nightfall, unloading operations had bogged down so badly that there was no choice but to bring them to a halt. The problem was solved in the morning by simply opening more protected beachfront for the temporary storage of supplies.

155mm artillery shells were off-loaded and stacked around a palm tree, destined for a nearby shore battery.

Japanese fighters attacked the transports during the unloadings. Tracer rounds are clearly visible as the hastily erected shore defenses swing into action. The invasion forces suffered minor damage from the attack.

8 AUGUST
THE BATTLE OF SAVO ISLAND

Within minutes of hearing about the American invasion, Japanese Admiral Gunichi Mikawa turned his fleet of warships towards the threatened islands. Using scout planes and intercepted radio traffic, Mikawa fixed the location of American ships near Savo Island. It took him only hours to prepare an attack and surprise the American fleet.

The key to Mikawa's plan was an assault at night. Night battles at sea were a new strategy, but the Japanese Navy had been well-trained. Using a proven combination of torpedoes and guns, his goal was to destroy the American warships off Savo, then turn around and sink their transports off Guadalcanal. Mikawa's strategy was unpredictably aggressive, and it caught the Americans off guard.

It was a tropical night without a moon, still and quiet until the seas pushed forth a terrifying monster. One Allied ship after another was caught by the beam of Japanese searchlights, then blasted with heat-accurate torpedoes and laced by five-inch shells.

By 0200, it was over. Four Allied ships had been sunk, with more than a thousand sailors disappearing under the blackened sea that would soon be known as Iron Bottom Sound. Feeling victorious but cautious, Admiral Mikawa decided to withdraw rather than risk an attack by the distant American aircraft carriers. Contrary to his original plan, he spared the American transports on this night.

A B-17 such as the one seen here over Gizo Island first spotted the oncoming Japanese force.

(Above) The night is broken by the flash of five-inch guns during training exercises just before the battle.

As dawn broke on August 9th, the truth was evident. The American destroyer force had been brutalized by the Japanese. Already sunk were the Astoria, Quincy *and* Vincennes, *as well as the Australian ship* Canberra. *The* Chicago, *seen at left just after the engagement, limps away, her stern low in the water. Over 1,000 sailors were dead. Marines on Guadalcanal saw and heard the engagement as they dug in for the night.*

27

8 AUGUST THE PUSH TO HENDERSON FIELD

After witnessing the lightning-like flashes of the night battle at sea, the Marines knew their test would come soon. Their mission was to push forward and capture the airfield. As they awakened and prepared to move inland, oil-covered bodies and dazed survivors from the night's naval action started washing ashore. It was an ominous sign.

Members of a Marine light tank unit survey their new territory. For them, the fighting is just about to begin.

A captured Japanese field artillery piece.

The Marine at right wears a captured Japanese sniper's jacket.

A Marine looks up at a Japanese sign left behind when the invasion began.

9 AUGUST
TAKING HENDERSON FIELD

After an excruciatingly slow march through the jungle, American forces secured the Japanese airfield on Guadalcanal and renamed it Henderson Field. Six days later it received its first operational unit, Marine Air Group 23. The newly arrived pilots in their F4F Wildcats engaged the enemy within 48 hours. Battles had now been waged at sea and in the sky. The next one would be on land.

The advantages of air superiority in this theater of the war were clear, and that is why both sides wanted to control the airfield on Guadalcanal. Started by the Japanese, the field was completed by American construction battalions, who lengthened it to nearly 4,000 feet. At first its runway was made of dirt and gravel, but metal matting was soon added to make a sturdier surface. The facility was named Henderson Field in honor of Major Lofton Henderson, a Marine aviator killed at Midway.

Report of the 5th Marines
August 8, 1942

0930 The First Battalion, supported by a tank company, crossed the Tango without opposition.

The Third Battalion continued to hold the left half of the beach-head in defense of the eastern sector of Red Beach. No enemy encountered.

1215 Enemy bombers and torpedo planes attacked our transports and screening ships off Red Beach. Hits observed on a destroyer and a transport.

1330 First Battalion reached airfield and found it undefended. There were quantities of building equipment, abandoned with no apparent effort at destruction.

The rapid advance of the 5th Marines seemed to speak well of the American forces, but their success was misleading. The Japanese had garrisoned only their engineering battalions on Guadalcanal, not their soldiers. The construction crews had fled quickly into the jungle at the first sound of incoming rounds. Having lost their most important asset in the Solomons, the Japanese were determined not to lose the island. The Americans were just as determined, setting the stage for months of ruthless fighting. At left, above, Marines inspect a Japanese anti-aircraft piece at the airfield. Bottom left, F4F Wildcats are parked on the ramp, ready to engage Japanese Zeroes. Above, the "Pagoda" was the most prominent structure on the field and was used for base operations.

The extent to which the enemy had been able to develop their positions was remarkable in view of the short time of occupation. Since 4 July they had succeeded in constructing large semi-permanent camps, finger wharves, bridges, machine shops, two large radio stations, ice plants, two large and permanent electric power plants, an elaborate air compressor plant for torpedoes and a nearly complete airdrome with hangers, blast pens and a 3,600-foot runway.

—After-action report

Marine Air Group 23 was a mixed bag of brand new pilots and pilots with experience at Midway. Their training had been rushed, as they had only recently been provided with the F4F Wildcats and SBD-3 dive bombers that would play a major part in the South Pacific air war. Still, their arrival at Henderson Field in August was good news for the Marines on the ground. Air power would play a role in almost every battle and would be essential in the non-stop attacks on Japanese re-supply barges and transports.

At right, a dive bomber (upper left) strafes a Japanese oil tank.

21 AUGUST
THE BATTLE OF TENARU

On this day the Japanese began their second counter-offensive. At 0200 Imperial Army Colonel Kiyoano Ichiki arrived on Guadalcanal with the 28th Infantry. Within 24 hours, Ichiki mounted an assault with a thousand soldiers. Following timeless battle tradition, Ichiki's forces struck at night, under the arc of a green flare and the startling cry of "*Banzai!*"

Even the experienced American Marines had never seen anything like it—wave after wave of Japanese soldiers, charging headlong through the Tenaru River lagoon into withering return fire. The Japanese surged across sandbars, eerily silhouetted by the light of battle, but they ran into and got tangled up by hidden strands of barbed wire. Machine gun and small-arms fire picked the Japanese lines apart, and tanks and artillery pounded their flanks. In less than two hours, there was total silence. Nearly 800 Japanese soldiers were dead.

As the acrid smell of gunpowder drifted across the lagoon and the Marines walked forward to survey the battlefield, they were bewildered not just by their victory, but by the tenacity of the enemy soldiers. Facing imminent death, only one had surrendered.

Automatic weapons proved to be an effective countermeasure for the type of mass attack the Japanese flung at U.S. troops at this battle. A V-shaped field of fire coordinated between shooting positions was the only way to stop the forward momentum of a banzai attack.

(Left) Barbed wire was strung to slow the Japanese attack. (Above) Withering fire from Marine rifle platoons left nearly 800 Japanese dead. The full extent of the carnage could not be assessed until the morning after. (Below) Marines practice with the .50 caliber machine gun that saved the day at Tenaru River.

The enemy reaction to our landing was to attack by air and sea and to alert and dispatch immediately to Guadalcanal the 2nd Division and two smaller units—the Ichiki and Kawaguchi forces. The Ichiki Detachment was first to land. This group amounted to well over 1,000 men. Deeming the force sufficient for its purposes, it was landed east of our beachhead and thrown against our left flank. Approximately 65 Marines held the sector in which the main forces attacked, and in the ensuing engagement, generally called the First Battle of Tenaru, the assault was repulsed with crippling losses, and the survivors were mopped up and scattered the next day.

—Official Marine Corps summary of the Battle of Tenaru. Tenaru exposed the newly arrived Marines to the first banzai attacks and the incredible willpower of the Japanese soldier. Nonetheless, barbed wire, well-placed machine guns, artillery and tanks brought fire to bear on the chilling charges of frenzied Japanese soldiers. Ichiki, the commanding officer, committed suicide following this tactical failure.

Much of the action of this battle occurred in a tidal lagoon near the beach. In the light of dawn, the dead were strewn over a wide area.

Marine corpsmen find a wounded Japanese soldier still alive following the Battle of Tenaru. His companions were not so lucky.

PATROLS

In 1942 there were no satellites to photograph enemy troop movements or concentrations. Even with reconnaissance aircraft available, the foot patrol was still the best way to gather intelligence on enemy activity. These patrols were demanding. In intense tropical heat, the men clawed through the thick foliage. Snipers were a constant threat. Marines typically gained a few miles, then collapsed from exhaustion. But they were the eyes and ears of the American command on Guadalcanal.

Another day, another patrol. Combat fatigue was a fact of life, caused by heat, bouts of malaria and dysentery, as well as the fear of snipers and sudden ambushes. Japanese soldiers dug tunnels and holes in the ground, popping up to fire at passing patrols. Occasionally the Yanks spotted and either caught or killed the sniper. At right, Marines drag an enemy soldier out of his hiding place.

(Far right, top) A bedraggled platoon takes a break on a ridge top before descending back into the jungle. (Far right, bottom) Securing a tunnel was harder than it looked. Hand grenades tossed into the holes would be thrown out. Tunnels turned sharply just beyond their entrances, providing protection from direct rifle fire. The solution was to tie TNT to a wooden plank, soak it in gasoline, and jam it in.

44

The sheer physical labor of moving through the tangled jungle undergrowth exhausted many patrols. Hills made it so tiring that it was easy to forget that the enemy could be five feet away.

There was an abundance of hardwood on the island, and it was perfect for building shelters, bridges and observation posts. Here a soldier wields an axe in a clearing.

A detachment of Marines marches toward the front from Henderson Field. Above them, a B-17 Flying Fortress takes off in search of Japanese targets.

Taking advantage of the dusk, companies will advance through the jungle (creeping on all fours if necessary) to the line at the edge of the forest and immediately assault the enemy position.

—From captured Japanese documents on the proper method for initiating an attack on the American forces

Japanese prisoners were not very numerous, especially in the early days of the campaign. Those who were taken alive were usually too sick or wounded to even commit suicide.

Australians made many contributions to the recapture of Guadalcanal. Most unusual among them were the coast watchers. Stationed in secret locations throughout the chain of islands forming the Solomons, they were the early-warning radar of the campaign. The pilots at Henderson Field would know within minutes when a flight of Zeroes took off from the main Japanese air base at Rabaul. The Japanese rarely attacked transports, warships or Henderson Field without prior knowledge by the Americans. (Right) This Australian has become a territorial "major."

Tactics, good medical support and artillery were the three main advantages the Americans had on Guadalcanal. The 75mm pack howitzers (left) were much feared by the Imperial Army.

(Below) Of all the Marine units sent to Guadalcanal, the artillery crews were the best trained and most experienced. Here Marines man a gun emplacement that was formerly held by the Japanese.

Two soldiers of the Americal Division are at the alert on the road leading to the front. Their 37mm anti-tank gun is camouflaged to knock out enemy tank columns. (Below) This field artillery battery is situated just below the crest of the ridge so it cannot be seen by the enemy. A camouflage net obscures it from the view of enemy aircraft.

24-25 AUGUST
BATTLE OF THE EASTERN SOLOMONS

Both sides in the Pacific relied heavily on re-supply convoys and troop transport ships. In late August, American intelligence learned that a large Japanese reinforcement fleet was sailing to Guadalcanal carrying the 35th Infantry Brigade and the 5th Special Naval Landing Force.

American naval forces prepared to unleash everything they had to stop this enemy fleet. Aircraft carriers, battleships, destroyers, and the land-based fighters and bombers from Henderson Field were called into action.

This Japanese counter-offensive began with a carrier battle. Planes from the USS *Enterprise* and USS *Saratoga* engaged the Japanese in the skies over the Solomons. Seventy-five Japanese planes fell, and the aircraft carrier *Ryujo* was sunk, at the price of 25 American planes.

At 0200 on 25 August, the battle focus shifted to the fast-approaching Japanese transports. American forces attacked the convoy with every measure they had, even with bombing runs by cumbersome B-17s. The results were impressive. The Japanese were forced to turn away, giving the Americans a decisive victory. The damaged aircraft carrier *Enterprise* retreated to Pearl Harbor for repairs.

Japanese dive bombers attack the carrier USS Enterprise. *(Above) The flaming wreckage of two of them can be seen very close to the ship's port side. (Below) This photograph shows the U.S. Navy Task Force 16 during the battle. The* Enterprise *is afire and has turned sharply to starboard to avoid being struck by a Japanese plane, which hits the water with a noticeable splash.*

(Right) In this aerial photograph, a Japanese cruiser (arrow at bottom right) is hit by a bomb dropped from a B-17. One bomb in a multi-bomb salvo hits the ship in the stern. A Japanese destroyer executes a high-speed starboard turn (arrow at top left) in a defensive maneuver.

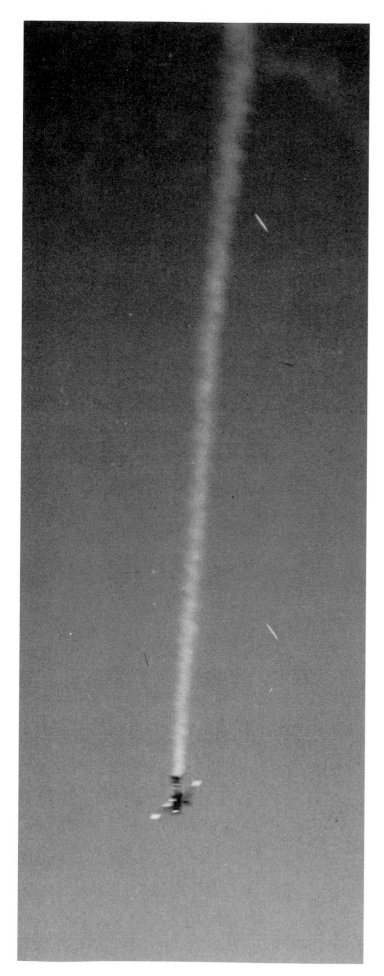

In the third aircraft carrier battle of World War II, the USS Enterprise *and the USS* Saratoga *moved into position to intercept the oncoming Japanese fleet, which included the carriers* Shokaku, Zuikaku *and* Ryujo. *One hundred and fifty-four American planes met 171 Japanese planes. Aichi D3A1 Vals catch fire (above and left) during a dive bombing run on the* Enterprise. *A bomb slams onto the* Enterprise's *flight deck (right). The* Enterprise *(below) was the prime target for attacking Japanese Zeroes.*

B-17 Flying Fortresses were deployed to Guadalcanal and had mixed results. Although they carried a considerable bomb load, they were better suited to the high-altitude raids of Europe than to the precision bombings of the Pacific. Nonetheless, their successes were measureable. (Below) A B-17 has scored a direct hit on the fantail of a Japanese troop transport, causing considerable damage and scattering the surrounding landing barges. The ship was later scuttled.

When I pulled up and looked around, I was just as scared as the Japs were. I noticed that there was a Zero dog-fighting with my wingman, and my wingman was keeping the Zero well occupied to keep from getting himself shot up. As I had about 500 feet altitude advantage on this Zero and he was right near me, it was no trouble at all – a ten-year-old kid could have just flown up his tail – and I shot him. But I couldn't get my wingman to join up even then. He headed for a cloud and got in it, so I thought it would be a good idea if I did the same. But about that time a Zero came up from below, shooting at me. Naturally, the ideal thing to do, or only thing to do, was to point down and start shooting at him. So I did. I had the same thing – a no-deflection shot with me on top. Well, with six .50 caliber guns going into a propeller and an engine, it's going to be disastrous no matter whose engine and whose propeller it is. The Jap's plane blew up pretty well with the pilot trying to get out. I suppose it lasted no more than three minutes.

—Major John L. Smith's after-action report. Smith, a Marine fighter pilot, describes two straight-on, "no deflection" air-to-air engagements that resulted in two victories for the Marine ace.

12-13 SEPTEMBER
THE BATTLE OF EDSON'S RIDGE

Through August and early September, the Japanese vigorously reinforced their island garrison with a naval operation known as the "Tokyo Express." At the same time, Americans on Guadalcanal entered dire straits. Daily air attacks and constant shelling whittled away their air strength and their nerves. Pathetic re-supply had left bone-weary Marines low on food and ammunition. The only troops they watched come and go were flying the flag of the Rising Sun.

After their setbacks at Tenaru River and the Eastern Solomons, the Japanese were now better prepared to retake Guadalcanal. Indeed, two-thousand, five-hundred Imperial Army soldiers had been quietly transported onto the island. Native scouts alerted the Americans of this Japanese build-up, but no one knew how many would attack, or when. The first shells fell on 12 August, in a half-hearted assault that was halted before morning.

On 13 August, as the sun dipped below the horizon, the main assault began in earnest on a 1,000-foot ridge only a mile from Henderson Field. The bloody night battle raged with unabated fury until dawn. Overwhelmed by the surging waves of Japanese soldiers, the Marines fell back, stumbling over the slaughtered bodies of friend and foe. With artillery, machine guns, pistols, and with their bare hands, they fought through the night. As dawn broke, the Marines had held their ground. But daylight also revealed hundreds of corpses, frozen in hand-to-hand combat, in gruesome testimony to the ferocity of the action. This blood-soaked ridge would later be named for Lt. Colonel Merritt A. Edson, the heroic Marine who led his forces through the hellish night of 13 September, and for it won a Medal of Honor.

When the enemy discovers even a single soldier, day or night, he concentrates his fire upon him. Therefore, we must take advantage of this, get him to waste his ammunition. In other words, we must set up a decoy where there are no troops distributed, flash a light at night, or use some other ingenious device.

For the full play of the power of cold steel, it is necessary to make a sudden attack upon the rear flank of the enemy's firepoint, leaning heavily on camouflage and the utilization of natural features. At this point, the enemy, brought at close quarters by our assault, will attempt to fire pistols and throw hand grenades.

—From captured Japanese documents, instructing the proper method for initiating an attack on Americans

This north-looking view shows the fighting position of the Marine Raiders along Edson's Ridge. Some Japanese elements attacked the Raiders from behind, hidden in the undergrowth visible on both sides of the Ridge. For a while the Raiders were cut off, but they forced a retreat and contact was reestablished on September 13.

15 SEPTEMBER
THE SINKING OF THE WASP

Japanese submarines discovered the aircraft carrier USS *Wasp* off Savo Island. Silently closing to 1,000 yards, they fired six torpedoes at the massive target, one of which slammed into her gasoline storage tank, while another detonated in a bomb magazine. Racked by explosions, *Wasp* listed fifteen degrees and began to sink. Captain Forrest Sherman issued the order to abandon ship, and the *Wasp* was lost in a stunning blow to the United States Navy.

The USS Wasp *(left) burns in the distance after being hit by torpedoes. It would soon sink. At right, the USS* O'Brien, *which also was hit, burns furiously, but survives.*

At right, the Wasp *lists to starboard, fatally wounded by torpedoes to her starboard gasoline hold and forward bomb magazine. The shock waves from these blasts set in motion a series of catastrophic explosions and fires that ship's firemen could not control. The ship was abandoned at 1520.*

18 SEPTEMBER
REINFORCEMENTS ARRIVE

The Japanese relied on fast convoy ships and troop barges to land reinforcements, moving mainly at night. The Americans preferred air convoys, saving their transports for larger operations. A daily task for Guadalcanal pilots and shore batteries, on both sides, was to attack each other's re-supply convoys.

During September and October, the Japanese and the Americans each landed major troop reinforcements. On 18 September, the 7th Marine Regiment landed at Lunga Point, with 4,000 Marines under the command of Lt. Col. Lewis "Chesty" Puller. They brought with them more ammunition and desperately needed fuel. Using the effective "Tokyo Express," the Japanese landed the 2nd Imperial Division. At this point in the conflict, American forces stood at 27,000 soldiers, Japanese at 30,000.

Landing boats full of Marines from a troop transport ship head for shore, peppered by gunfire from three Japanese planes (upper right). Interdiction of reinforcements was a key component of both American and Japanese strategies for taking the island.

(Left) This air view shows the Marine landing at Lunga Point in mid-September. Higgins boats wait their turn to hit the beach.

American air power draws a bead on Japanese reinforcement efforts, scoring a hit on a troop ship. In the distance, fires burn from another bombing. The so-called Tokyo Express was successful in evading American ships and airplanes, bringing thousands of troops, tanks, ammunition rounds and food items to the island by night. Daylight runs were not so successful. Scores of Japanese freighters and troop ships wound up sunk and grounded, like the Kyushu Maru *at right.*

After the initial failures, the enemy realized that a larger force was needed to drive us from the island. The 2nd Imperial Division landed on Guadalcanal during September and early October 1942. The division reached shore almost intact with considerable reinforcements and heavy equipment, including tanks, and totaled over 20,000 men. It was principally troops from this division that opposed our push from the Lunga River to the Matanikau.

—Marine history

Marauding Japanese planes found a target of opportunity in a U.S. ship unloading near Lunga Beach. (Top) LST #340 is struck in its gas tanks, causing a massive explosion. (Bottom) LCT #58 comes alongside and turns its fire-fighting hoses on the burning ship.

The black bursts of intense American anti-aircraft fire surround four Japanese bombers coming in extremely low to attack U.S. transports at far left.

A low-flying U.S. Navy Douglas Dauntless surveys the damage done to two Japanese transports by dive bombers.

Battle debris. The remains of a Japanese light tank hit by American planes before it could reach the shelter of the jungle.

(Right) Once ashore, American soldiers organized by unit, consolidating their equipment into specific areas. The heat, moisture and mildew of the tropical climate played havoc with radios, rifles and motor vehicles, making re-supply a constant need. A Guadalcanal native is visible, helping his American friends. The natives had been harshly treated by the Japanese, and were only too glad to serve as lookouts and scouts for the Americans.

SEPTEMBER-OCTOBER MATANIKAU RIVER ACTIONS

Five miles from the American beaches at Lunga Point was the Matanikau River, beyond which Imperial soldiers disappeared into the jungle and reformed their units. This area was also a staging ground for the newly-arrived Imperial Army reinforcements, deposited there by the "Tokyo Express" convoys.

The Matanikau was a natural defensive barrier, and the Marines considered its integrity essential to the security of Henderson Field. In late September, General Vandegrift ordered Lt. Colonel Puller to clean out the Japanese hiding in the jungles across the river. Puller conducted several raids, and his engagements were small but bloody. In October, as the new Japanese troops moved toward the river to establish an encampment, Puller's forces, as well as Edson's, engaged them in several particularly vicious battles. Sixty-five Americans were killed, as were more than 600 Japanese.

Traversing the rivers, streams and lagoons of Guadalcanal was often accomplished in an imaginative way. These Marines cross the Matanikau on a wooden raft that has been rigged as a makeshift ferry. (Below) The Matanikau River, dubbed "Bloody River" after a series of battles in the fall of 1942.

During the battle of Matanikau River, Marine casualties were sometimes transported to the rear by boat, pushed and paddled through the shallow parts and rapids of the river. Boats coming the other way were headed for the front lines on the ridgetops, loaded with supplies and ammunition dropped in the rear by airplanes.

During a lull in the fighting, a Marine does a little housecleaning—he hangs his wet clothes out to dry, and reloads his automatic weapon belt.

Reinforcements head for the front to relieve Marine units at the Matanikau River.

A Marine mortar squad fires shells into Japanese positions from the underside of a ridge during the offensive west of the Matanikau River.

It was easier to go up and down the rivers than through the jungle, which was why keeping both banks clear of the enemy was so important.

A G.I. uses a captured Japanese light machine gun as his personal weapon.

One tank, in delivering effective fire into the Jap positions, got ahead of its supporting troops. The Japanese rushed out of their dugouts and caves and stalled it by inserting a large bar into the track. In attempting to free this bar, the tank backed into a stump of a coconut tree and became lodged thereon with the overhanging portion of the rear of the tank, thus preventing any forward or rearward movement of the tank. The Japanese threw Molotov cocktails and other flammables, which killed the entire crew with the exception of one man, who managed to escape.

—After-action report

In the pre-Sherman days of World War II, the armor inventory of both the Army and Marines was noticeably small. But light tanks did fine in the mud and sand of Guadalcanal, even if their firepower was puny by world standards. (Left) Americans, too, utilized the talents of snipers in the South Pacific. Here two of them use native vegetation to accomplish the sniper's first objective: concealment.

11-12 OCTOBER THE BATTLE OF CAPE ESPERANCE

At this time, two reinforcement actions were underway. The Imperial Japanese Navy was in the process of landing heavy artillery and fresh reinforcements onto Guadalcanal, just as the United States Navy approached with the 164th Infantry Regiment of the Army's Americal Division.

The Japanese quickly moved to interdict the Americans, just off the northern coast. But it was not easy. The American convoy escort included nine warships and the carrier USS *Hornet*. The Japanese first attacked Henderson Field, hoping to destroy the main American fighter force before engaging the ships. Japanese Zeroes and "Betty" long-range bombers attacked at high noon on 11 October. Fifty American fighters took to the air and repelled them.

Meanwhile, at sea, the Americans were determined to get through. They had learned from the Savo battle that their warships must be prepared to engage the Japanese at any time, and particularly at night. At 2200 hours on 11 October, the first shots were fired. Two hours later, four new Japanese warships were sunk in Iron Bottom Sound. These clashes did not halt the Japanese off-loading of new artillery pieces, but it helped secure the landing of 2,850 American Army soldiers on 13 October.

A "cease fire" call puts an end to a day of artillery barrages for these Marines. The 75mm gun howitzer is about to have a canvas muzzle put over its barrel to protect it as much as possible from rain, rust and dirt.

Henderson Field was the target of bombing attacks in the early stages of the battle. Bomb craters are clearly visible in the foreground.

(Right) Marines gaze skyward from the door of their air raid shelter near Henderson Field.

As this photograph demonstrates, the power of naval ordnance is more than even steel superstructures can stand. Shell fragments from the Kinugasa during the Battle of Cape Esperance have penetrated this crew compartment on board the USS Boise. A Kinugasa eight-inch shell penetrated the hull of the Boise, setting off a massive explosion of stored gunpowder that killed 100 men. (Right) The USS San Francisco, one of the heroes of the Battle of Cape Esperance. It was from the bridge of this ship, flagship of the fleet that included Vincennes, Astoria and Quincy, that Rear Admiral Norman Scott managed to defeat the Japanese at their own game—a close-quarters night engagement.

24-26 OCTOBER
THE BATTLE FOR
HENDERSON FIELD

With both sides reinforced, the opening salvos of a major confrontation fell on 18 October. Using their new artillery, the Japanese began shelling Henderson Field. To the north, Imperial Army troops maneuvered into battle formations. These tactics, however, were merely a diversion to keep the Americans focused on the northern approaches. The Americans were unaware that the Japanese were hacking their way through the dense jungle around their southern flank.

The perimeter of Henderson Field was once again the battleground on 24 October. The Japanese attacked, and Lt. Col. Puller's men quickly turned toward the charge and opened fire. Japanese soldiers were held up by barbed wire, and their bodies were raked by machine gun and small-arms fire. By morning, 300 Japanese soldiers were dead. Sixty men successfully infiltrated the American lines, but they were eventually discovered and killed.

Later that day, fighter planes from Henderson Field took to the sky and attacked Imperial Navy ships as they moved into position to shell again. The planes were met by a swarm of incoming Zeroes, and a massive dogfight ensued. On the ground, Puller understood what this vigorous aerial defense meant: he had yet to face a real ground assault.

Beginning at 2000 hours, Puller's men faced the most intense combat of the war. They held the line, but 86 Americans were killed. The Marines estimated the Japanese dead at 2,200.

Forces that have attacked landing fields should endeavor to take planes, gasoline, etc., with as little damage as possible. Therefore, in order to prevent the planes from escaping, and so as to not start fires from the gasoline, they should merely damage the tires without damage to the plane.

—From captured Japanese documents

Japanese planes score a direct hit on a hangar at Henderson Field. White smoke pours from the damaged building. The aircraft barely visible on the apron appear to have escaped damage. (Below) During a Japanese bombardment of Henderson Field, ground crews wheeled this Marine dive bomber under a coconut grove for concealment. Luck was not with them, however, as a bomb struck the plane directly, smashing it to pieces.

Henderson Field's runways were 150 feet wide—a bit narrow for the B-17s but adequate for Marine fighter-bombers. The strip ran east to west, ending abruptly near the Lunga River. Here an F4F Wildcat starts its takeoff run. (Below) Shore watchers and reconnaissance planes would alert Henderson Field if Japanese Zeroes were spotted on an inbound raid. The American pilots would scramble to meet the incoming force. A Japanese strategy was to send a second wave of airplanes behind the first, timed to arrive when the Americans landed to refuel.

Our doctrine was to attack.

The Japs would catch fire very readily; sometimes they would even blow up. Sometimes they would just drop out of formation and glide down and go into the water.

Although they were hitting the field every day and made many hits on the runway, the engineers would fill up the hole and you'd be landing 15 minutes later.

—Major John L. Smith's after-action interview

Japanese air raids claim another hangar. By the time the enemy bombers were overhead, most airplanes and personnel had dispersed to the fringes of the airfield, hidden in the palm trees. But the buildings and runway were fair game, and construction crews were constantly rebuilding hangars and filling bomb craters.

26 OCTOBER
NAVY BATTLE OF SANTA CRUZ

The Imperial Navy planned to support the Battle of Henderson Field by blocking the sea lanes with their own aircraft carriers, thereby preventing U.S. warships from coming to the aid of the Marines on Guadalcanal. This plan, however, changed. Slowed by the dense jungle, the ground soldiers fell several days behind schedule. During this delay, the American aircraft carrier USS *Enterprise* arrived on the scene. A powerful American Navy was suddenly looming in the background. Admiral Isoroku Yamamato, commander of the Imperial forces, sensed the threat and seized an opportunity. Yamamoto ordered his navy to turn and attack.

Having learned their lessons from Midway, the Japanese launched their planes first. In a swirling beehive of fighters, torpedo bombers and attack bombers, the rival air fleets engaged in an aerial fight that lasted for hours. The Japanese stayed on the offensive, and the air battles slowly moved over the U.S. carriers. Black puffs of anti-aircraft fire dotted the skies as the carrier USS *Hornet* became the focus of the bombers. Hit by two torpedoes, five bombs and at least two kamikaze strikes, the *Hornet* finally went down.

Low on fuel, Yamamato ordered his fleet to retreat. The U.S. Navy lost two ships and suffered damage to eleven others. The Americans lost more than 80 airplanes, the Japanese 97. The fourth carrier battle of World War II was a defeat for the U.S. Navy. But there was one saving grace: once again, an attack on Henderson Field had been blunted.

The USS Hornet *is afire and seriously damaged near its signal bridge. (Below) A photographer aboard the USS* San Juan *captured the furious attack on the USS* Enterprise. *An explosion has shaken the carrier so hard that a Dauntless is jarred off the flight deck.*

The USS Northampton *tows the* Hornet *just before she had to cut loose because Japanese planes attacked.*

The Hornet's *last moments. Torpedo planes circle the wounded carrier as a dive bomber is about to crash onto the carrier's island. Bomb damage is visible on the aft portion of the ship.*

The dive bomber crashes into the Hornet's *signal bridge. Unable to regain power after this strike, and listing at nearly 15 degrees, the ship had to be abandoned. (Below) Two Japanese bombers look for targets, flying between a battleship on the left and a fast-departing ship on the right that leaves a swerving wake from a high-speed turn.*

The dive bomber attack on the Enterprise, *as seen from the USS* Portland. *The carrier is listing some 15 degrees, but damage control crews can still be seen on the flight deck.*

Photographed from the USS Pensacola, *a Japanese torpedo bomber heads straight for the immobile* Hornet. *(Below) The plane has dropped its torpedo, which splashes short of the target. Shortly after this photograph was taken, another torpedo found the mark, striking the* Hornet *on its starboard side just aft of a previous hit.*

Even in the Hornet's *death throes, its crew works frantically to save the ship. Here on the flight deck, with fire, acrid smoke and the wreckage of Japanese dive bombers hindering movement, damage control teams man high-pressure water hoses to quench the flames.*

IN THE JUNGLE

Historians, novelists and filmmakers have all treated the Guadalcanal jungles as the third antagonist in the Solomons campaign. As any veteran will attest, it was more than just a dark, oppressive backdrop for military actions; it killed people on both sides. Malaria incapacitated more soldiers than bullets did.

It has been speculated that the American forces coped with the jungle's hazards better than the Japanese, and that environmental management gave them a decisive edge. Perhaps that is so. But no soldier felt that way about it at the time. For them, it was just one day in hell after another. And at night–that's when the enemy started fighting.

As the Japanese soldiers had before them, U.S. soldiers found the hollowed-out roots of hardwood trees a great place to hide when the mortar barrages started.

102

After a while, being wet and tired stopped being a new experience for the American Marine. Here, in a tropical downpour, GIs unload a landing boat. (Below left) Dawn in the jungle. The tropical sun filters through the trees, throwing shafts of light on the jungle floor. It would be beautiful, if not for the insects, mosquitoes, snakes and fungi.

Among American troops, malaria appeared alarmingly in September, and the reported incidence rose rapidly so as to incapacitate about 15 percent of the force during November. Thereafter, it fell slightly, those hospitalized remaining at around 10 percent till the end of the campaign. Diarrhea was also prevalent at intervals, particularly in one regiment. The cumulative effect of these conditions was grave. A significant percentage of our forces was out of action much of the time and our military effectiveness was reduced. The result, however, was never quite serious enough to prevent the troops from dealing with enemy assaults successfully and from making such counter-attacks as were necessary.

—Official Marine report

Like laundry on the line, canvas machine gun belts hang out to dry and to be reloaded. Thirty and .50 caliber machine guns and the crews that manned them were a Marine Corps specialty, and proved invaluable in the kind of defensive warfare U.S. troops employed.

Even in a jungle clearing, a cook needs a place to work. This makeshift kitchen provided enough hot food and coffee to keep the troops moving. When the fighting got close, even the cooks grabbed rifles in the best Marine Corps tradition ("Every Marine is a rifleman")

Members of the 3rd Defense Battalion pose with a wing from a Japanese bomber they shot down with their 90mm anti-aircraft gun.

A Marine sentry area near Henderson Field. This soldier has the ideal setup—a tent for quiet times, a ready foxhole for when the shelling starts, and a rifle and two grenades if the Japanese get close.

The Japanese operated in dense jungles and swampy areas. We chose open country, coconut groves or grassy ridges wherever we could. Their troops had little or no motor transport, and became exhausted from long marches with heavy loads. The Japanese were never able to set up a smoothly functioning field hospital, and the sick who were treated were ordinarily laid out on mats or on the ground in the jungle, and sometimes given some scant shelter by means of palm thatch. Sanitation in these outdoor sickbays was atrocious. The sick were reluctant to use trench latrines, particularly at night, and deposited their excrement in the immediate vicinity of their mats, whence it was often washed into the lean-to shelters by the rain. Food was extremely scarce, and coconuts, grass, taro, wild potatoes, fern and bamboo sprouts, and even crocodile and lizards, were used as emergency sources of nourishment. Miserable, without shelter, soaked with the rain, underfed, with little hope of evacuation, and bitten continuously by mosquitoes, it is no wonder the Japanese died in large numbers.

—A Marine Corps evaluation

To rig a hard-wire communications system, Marines strung telephone wire all over the island, using hardwood trees as telephone poles. (Below) Going point-to-point was the shortest way, and this often involved hand-carrying wires across streams.

(Right) There were uncounted tales of heroism among marines manning machine guns along the ridgelines. Several marines earned the Medal of Honor for single-handedly holding off waves of Japanese attacking by night. In the morning, having a cup of coffee and being alive were reward enough.

(Right) A jungle trail was often no wider than a Jeep. In tree-lined "canyons" such as this, American troops were vulnerable to sniper attack.

(Left) Motor vehicles as well as men get a much-needed bath. The rivers of Guadalcanal were fresh and clean, except for when the occasional dead Japanese soldier floated by.

This air raid warning bell is made from a Japanese artillery shell.

(Left) An Army officer uses a loud speaker (placed facing enemy lines, in picture above) to broadcast a "surrender or be killed" message to remaining Japanese troops. This ultimatum was not wishful thinking; by late fall of 1942, the Japanese garrison had been nearly wiped out. After losses of some 20,000 men, Japanese officers fled the island, leaving the sick and wounded behind.

In a propaganda move of their own, the Japanese dropped these "tickets to armistice" over U.S. lines to tempt American soldiers into surrendering. The tantalizing offer was ignored; the pictures were probably kept.

TICKET TO ARMISTICE

USE THIS TICKET, SAVE YOUR LIFE
YOU WILL BE KINDLY TREATED

Follow These Instructions:

1. Come towards our lines waving a white flag.
2. Strap your gun over your left shoulder muzzle down and pointed behind you.
3. Show this ticket to the sentry.
4. Any number of you may surrender with this one ticket.

JAPANESE ARMY HEADQUARTERS

投 降 票

此ノ票ヲ持ツモノハ投降者ナリ
投降者ヲ殺害スルヲ嚴禁ス

大日本軍司令官

Sing your way to Peace pray for Peace

The relative tranquility of daylight could be interrupted at any moment. Imperial Navy ships often trained their guns on the troops at Henderson Field. The "Mosquito Network" communications center on the island, which was usually evacuated during shellings, took a direct hit during one of these bombardments. Wooden splinters were all that remained when the "all clear" signal was given.

12-15 NOVEMBER
NAVAL BATTLE OF GUADALCANAL

In November, both navies ferried convoys of reinforcements to Guadalcanal. The Americans arrived on 12 November, unloading 5,500 men on Lunga Beach without incident. Six hundred miles away, 7,000 Imperial soldiers boarded Japanese transports while an advance fleet of destroyers and cruisers headed out to shell Henderson Field.

The U.S. Navy learned that the Japanese destroyers were on their way, and although severely outgunned, the Americans quickly escorted their transports to safety, then bravely turned around to intercept the enemy. As darkness fell on the night of 12 November, the opposing ships confronted each other, engaging in furious point-blank fire. Shells slammed one after another, sometimes streaking over the bow of one ship only to blast the superstructure of another. It was a brutal engagement for both sides, but it was clearly won by the Japanese. Five American and three Japanese ships went down, along with more than 2,000 sailors.

On shore, Henderson Field was spared, but the nearby flashes of the naval battle were disquieting. Sleep came in fits. As morning dawned, the sea was quiet, but not for long.

Yamamato again dispatched his fast cruisers to Guadalcanal and, in the early hours of 14 November, they did what they couldn't do the day before. They successfully shelled Henderson Field. American fighter planes scrambled to get airborne and score hits, as did airplanes launched from the *Enterprise*.

As the Japanese reinforcement convoy set sail, Admiral William F. "Bull" Halsey, commander of the American naval forces, ordered his battleships to Savo Island. The waters were soon crowded with warships and transports, and the pilots from Henderson and *Enterprise* attacked them unopposed. Darting amid the Japanese ships, the American planes picked their targets and bombed away, sinking six transports and turning away three more.

Fourteen Japanese warships were still approaching Savo Island and, as the sun went down on 13 November, the American battleships were ready. Once again, the night fighting was a terrifying cacaphony of guns and bombs. By dawn, eight American vessels and 23 Japanese ships had sunk to the bottom of Iron Bottom Sound.

This was the decisive moment. The Japanese command realized it could not dislodge the Americans from Guadalcanal.

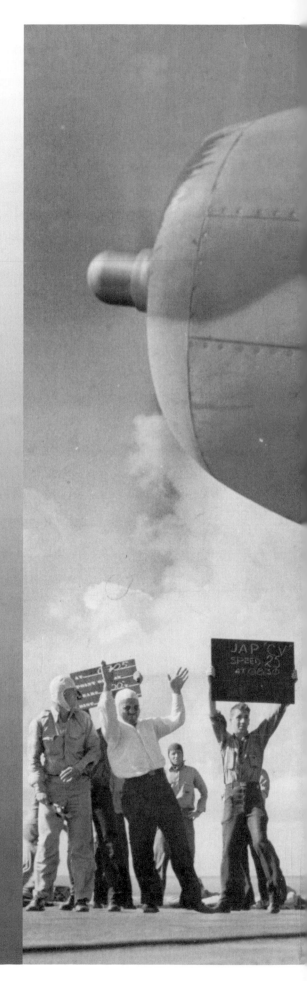

*(Above) Carrier flight operations,
especially in the middle of a
major battle, are never dainty.
The name of the game is to get in
the air, fight, land, refuel, and
fight again. Sometimes, in haste,
accidents happen. Here a Wildcat
hits the flight deck too hard,
crumpling its landing gear.*

*(Right)Anti-aircraft batteries put
up a wall of flak to knock down
Japanese torpedo planes, as seen
from the deck of the USS*
President Adams.

The night strike on Henderson Field claims another U.S. aircraft.

Anti-aircraft fire brings down a Japanese dive bomber, whose pilot tries to steer into a U.S. vessel. On this night, he missed.

A gunner aboard the Enterprise *scans the sky for targets. His challenge is to spot low-flying planes and knock them out of the sky before they can drop torpedoes or ram themselves into his ship.*

30 NOVEMBER
THE BATTLE OF
TASSAFARONGA

As November drew to a close, 20,000 Japanese ground troops on Guadalcanal were nearing starvation. They had been using submarines as resupply transports, which proved inadequate for the job. Rear Admiral Raizo Tanaka was charged with leading eight destroyers as a reinforcement unit to deliver several thousand drums of barley and rice to the weakened garrison.

At 2325, several American cruisers closed on the Japanese convoy off Tassafaronga and started to fire. The *Takanami*, in front, took most of the hits, but several destroyers sneaked past, hidden in the blackness of the fringe of the convoy. Rather than continue toward the island, however, the Japanese destroyers turned and fired a total of 44 Long Lance torpedoes at the American ships. One after another, they were hit—the *Minneapolis*, the *New Orleans* and the *Pensacola*—with nearly 400 crewmen and officers killed. The *Takanami* finally sank with 210 of its crew, and soon the *Northampton* was also sunk. In the end, the Japanese lost four destroyers and were prevented from making their resupply delivery. But once again they succeeded in demolishing a superior American fleet in a face-to-face naval confrontation.

Two enemy planes, punched out by gunners on the USS President Adams, *hit the water between the USS* Libra *and the USS* Betelguese

As soon as the drive westward showed signs of success, the Japanese realized that the campaign was lost, and their evacuation of survivors commenced in January. Destroyers and barges were run to Cape Esperance, and those who could make their way that far along the coast were taken to Bougainville as fast as the capacity of available transportation allowed. Most of the surviving Japanese General and Field Officers left by this means, deserting the remnants of their commands. The bulk of the evacuation was accomplished in three nights, using about 20 destroyers each night. Only one of these ships was lost during the evacuation.

—Marine after-action report

A fallen Marine gets the hand-written epitaph, "Here lies a Devil Dog."

(Both above) Japanese prisoners taken during the last few days of fighting on the island. There weren't many. Some of the Japanese wounded had been left behind when the Japanese army evacuated the island. Many of them died before U.S. medical aid could reach them. Others, though wounded, chose to fight to the death rather than surrender.

AFTERMATH

A small cemetery, ordained with simple wooden crosses etched with crudely inked epitaphs, was established near Henderson Field. Hundreds of men were interred there, awaiting removal to permanent graves in the United States. As December arrived on Guadalcanal, the island was deemed secure enough to evacuate the 1st Marine Division. Replacement troops would carry the battle to its final conclusion and the Japanese withdrawal on February 3rd. But for now, the men of the 1st Marines were leaving, and they had friends to whom they wished to say goodbye. One by one, singly and in pairs, they drifted over to the cemetery.

World War II continued for two and a half years before the Japanese surrendered in Tokyo Bay. Bitter battles would be fought throughout the islands of the Pacific. Guadalcanal, though, was the first victory. On the ground, 1,598 men were killed, 1,152 of them marines. The wounded totaled 4,709, with 2,799 of them marines. At sea, 5,041 died, 2,953 were wounded. On their side, the Japanese suffered 25,000 dead, half from combat, half from disease and starvation.

Marine General Vandegrift, who led the combined land forces, was awarded the Medal of Honor by President Roosevelt. The 1st Marine Division won the Presidential Unit Citation. After months of daily press coverage, the Guadalcanal victory, when it came, was celebrated wildly on the home front.

Admiral Halsey, known for colorful language and common-sense wit, put Guadalcanal into perspective: "Before Guadalcanal, the enemy advanced at his pleasure. After Guadalcanal, he retreated at ours."

By January 1943, the Marines had been relieved by U.S. Army regulars, and the wounded could start being taken to waiting hospital ships. In six months of fighting on land, sea and air, over 7,000 allied fighting men had died (or were missing) in the Guadalcanal theater. Nearly 2000 men had died in the jungles of Guadalcanal.

After Guadalcanal, several years of fighting remained in the South Pacific. But the lessons learned at Guadalcanal would guide U.S. forces all the way to Tokyo. Some of those lessons were in battlefield medicine, especially in a tropical climate. The effects of malaria, for example, sidelined as many Americans as enemy bullets until eradication methods and vaccines were developed. Corpsmen also gained valuable experience with emergency field dressings and traumatic wound treatment under the harshest conditions, which undoubtedly saved many lives at Kwajalein, Iwo Jima and Corregidor.

Henderson Field, once it was securely in U.S. control, became home base for air operations in the south Solomon Islands area. As the Marines moved north through other island chains, new airfields were either captured or created, forming a stepping-stone path of airfields from which U.S. air power could be trained on Japan. It was bulldozer power—the ability to build working airfields out of the jungle—as much as aircraft engine power that made it happen, and it all started on Guadalcanal.

After being there for a day or two, we got a pretty good idea of the tactics the Japanese bombers used. They always came over between 11 and 2:30, and the watchers told us when they were coming over, how many bombers there were, and how many fighters there were. You can see that we had them at a great disadvantage, (1) knowing exactly when they were coming, and (2) fighting over our own airfield. If they shot one of us down, and the plane didn't burn, we went in and had a dead-stick landing on the field. If the plane burned, our pilots jumped out over the field and were saved.

—Major Smith's after-action report

Marines muster to get off Guadalcanal the way they came in—on landing boats. They carry what's left of their belongings on their backs—a light load after six months of fighting. Ahead of them were many months and thousands of miles of tough going, just as it had been on Guadalcanal.

The commanders of the action at Guadalcanal convened there in January 1943. Standing at an observation post that looks down upon the precious terrain that claimed nearly 2,000 American lives are, left to right, Secretary of the Navy Frank Knox; Maj. Gen. Alexander M. Patch, Jr.; Admiral Chester W. Nimitz, Commander of the Pacific Fleet; William F. "Bull" Halsey, Commander of the South Pacific Fleet; and Maj. Gen. J. Lawton Collins.

"Before Guadalcanal the enemy advanced at his pleasure.
After Guadalcanal, he retreated at ours."
—*Admiral William F. "Bull" Halsey*